AF188458

Impressum
Verlag: BABADADA GmbH, Nedderfeld 112 , 22529 Hamburg
Geschäftsführer / Verlagsleitung: Harald Hof
Druck: Books on Demand GmbH, In de Tarpen 42, 22848 Norderstedt

Imprint
Publisher: BABADADA GmbH, Nedderfeld 112 , 22529 Hamburg, Germany
Managing Director / Publishing direction: Harald Hof
Print: Books on Demand GmbH, In de Tarpen 42, 22848 Norderstedt

divide
dividieren

186/2

board
Tafel

classroom
Klassenzimmer

school yard
Schulhof

teacher
Lehrer

paper
Papier

write
schreiben

pen
Stift

desk
Schreibtisch

ruler
Lineal

book
Buch

pupil
Schüler

satchel

Ranzen

pencil case

Federmappe

pencil

Bleistift

pencil sharpener

Bleistiftanspitzer

rubber

Radiergummi

drawing pad

Zeichenblock

drawing

Zeichnung

paintbrush

Pinsel

paint box

Malkasten

scissors

Schere

glue

Klebstoff

exercise book

Übungsheft

homework

Hausaufgabe

number

Zahl

2+2

add

addieren

subtract

subtrahieren

multiply

multiplizieren

calculate

rechnen

letter

Buchstabe

alphabet

Alphabet

word

Wort

text

Text

read

lesen

chalk

Kreide

lesson

Stunde

register

Klassenbuch

examination

Prüfung

certificate

Zeugnis

school uniform

Schuluniform

education

Ausbildung

encyclopedia

Lexikon

university

Universität

microscope

Mikroskop

map

Karte

waste-paper basket

Papierkorb

hotel
Hotel

hostel
Herberge

currency exchange office
Wechselstube

car
Auto

language

Sprache

yes / no

ja / nein

Okay

Okay

hello

Hallo

translator

Übersetzer

Thank you

Danke

how much is...?

Was kostet...?

I don´t get it

Ich verstehe nicht

problem

Problem

Good evening!

Guten Abend!

Good morning!

Guten Morgen!

Good night!

Gute Nacht!

goodbye

Auf Wiedersehen

direction

Richtung

luggage

Gepäck

bag

Tasche

backpack

Rucksack

guest

Gast

room

Zimmer

sleeping bag

Schlafsack

tent

Zelt

tourist information

Touristeninformation

beach

Strand

credit card

Kreditkarte

breakfast

Frühstück

lunch

Mittagessen

dinner

Abendessen

Ticket

Fahrkarte

elevator

Fahrstuhl

stamp

Briefmarke

border

Grenze

customs

Zoll

embassy

Botschaft

visa

Visum

passport

Pass

airplane
Flugzeug

ship
Schiff

fire truck
Feuerwehrauto

bus
Bus

truck
Lastwagen

motorboat
Motorboot

bike
Fahrrad

car
Auto

ferry

Fähre

boat

Boot

motorbike

Motorrad

police car

Polizeiauto

racing car

Rennauto

rental car

Mietwagen

car sharing

Carsharing

tow truck

Abschleppwagen

garbage truck

Müllauto

engine

Motor

fuel

Kraftstoff

fuel station

Tankstelle

traffic sign

Verkehrsschild

traffic

Verkehr

traffic jam

Stau

parking lot

Parkplatz

train station

Bahnhof

tracks

Schienen

train

Zug

tram

Straßenbahn

wagon

Wagon

helicopter

Helikopter

airport

Flughafen

tower

Tower

passenger

Passagier

container

Container

carton

Karton

cart

Karren

basket

Korb

take off / land

starten / landen

city
Stadt

village

Dorf

city center

Stadtzentrum

house

Haus

movie theater
Kino

advert
Werbung

street light
Straßenlaterne

CINEMA

street
Straße

taxi
Taxi

snack shop
Kiosk

pedestrian
Fußgänger

sidewalk
Bürgersteig

zebra crossing
Zebrastreifen

dumpster
Mülltonne

crossing
Kreuzung

traffic lights
Ampel

hut

Hütte

apartment

Wohnung

train station

Bahnhof

city hall

Rathaus

museum

Museum

school

Schule

university

Universität

bank

Bank

hospital

Krankenhaus

hotel

Hotel

pharmacy

Apotheke

office

Büro

book shop

Buchhandlung

shop

Geschäft

flower shop

Blumenladen

supermarket

Supermarkt

market

Markt

department store

Kaufhaus

fishmonger's shop

Fischhändler

mall

Einkaufszentrum

harbor

Hafen

park

Park

bench

Bank

bridge

Brücke

stairs

Treppe

subway

U-Bahn

tunnel

Tunnel

bus stop

Bushaltestelle

bar

Bar

restaurant

Restaurant

postbox

Briefkasten

street sign

Straßenschild

parking meter

Parkuhr

zoo

Zoo

swimming pool

Badeanstalt

mosque

Moschee

farm
Bauernhof

pollution
Umweltverschmutzung

cemetery
Friedhof

church
Kirche

playground
Spielplatz

temple
Tempel

landscape
Landschaft

signpost
Wegweiser

path
Weg

meadow
Wiese

stone
Stein

tree
Baum

hiker
Wanderer

river
Fluss

grass
Gras

flower
Blume

valley

Tal

hill

Berg

lake

See

forest

Wald

desert

Wüste

volcano

Vulkan

castle

Schloss

rainbow

Regenbogen

mushroom

Pilz

palm tree

Palme

mosquito

Moskito

fly

Fliege

ant

Ameise

bee

Biene

spider

Spinne

beetle

Käfer

frog

Frosch

squirrel

Eichhörnchen

hedgehog

Igel

hare

Hase

owl

Eule

bird

Vogel

swan

Schwan

boar

Wildschwein

deer

Hirsch

moose

Elch

dam

Staudamm

wind turbine

Windrad

solar panel

Solarmodul

climate

Klima

landscape - Landschaft

waiter
Kellner

menu
Speisekarte

chair
Stuhl

soup
Suppe

pizza
Pizza

cutlery
Besteck

tablecloth
Tischdecke

starter

Vorspeise

main course

Hauptgericht

dessert

Nachspeise

drinks

Getränke

food

Essen

bottle

Flasche

fast food

Fastfood

street food

Streetfood

teapot

Teekanne

sugar bowl

Zuckerdose

portion

Portion

espresso machine

Espressomaschine

high chair

Hochstuhl

bill

Rechnung

tray

Tablett

knife

Messer

fork

Gabel

spoon

Löffel

teaspoon

Teelöffel

serviette

Serviette

glass

Glas

plate

Teller

soup plate

Suppenteller

saucer

Untertasse

sauce

Sauce

salt shaker

Salzstreuer

pepper mill

Pfeffermühle

vinegar

Essig

oil

Öl

spices

Gewürze

ketchup

Ketchup

mustard

Senf

mayonnaise

Mayonnaise

special offer
Angebot

customer
Kunde

dairy products
Milchprodukte

shopping cart
Einkaufswagen

FOR

fruit
Obst

butcher's shop
Schlachterei

bakery
Bäckerei

weigh
wiegen

vegetables
Gemüse

meat
Fleisch

frozen food
Tiefkühlkost

cold cuts

Aufschnitt

canned food

Konserven

detergent

Waschmittel

candy

Süßigkeiten

household products

Haushaltsartikel

cleaning products

Reinigungsmittel

sales representative

Verkäuferin

cash register

Kasse

cashier

Kassierer

shopping list

Einkaufsliste

opening hours

Öffnungszeiten

wallet

Brieftasche

credit card

Kreditkarte

bag

Tasche

plastic bag

Plastiktüte

Getränke

water

Wasser

juice

Saft

milk

Milch

coke

Cola

wine

Wein

beer

Bier

alcohol

Alkohol

cocoa

Kakao

tea

Tee

coffee

Kaffee

espresso

Espresso

cappuccino

Cappuccino

banana

Banane

apple

Apfel

orange

Orange

melon

Melone

lemon

Zitrone

carrot

Karotte

garlic

Knoblauch

bamboo

Bambus

onion

Zwiebel

mushroom

Pilz

nuts

Nüsse

noodles

Nudeln

spaghetti

Spaghetti

rice

Reis

salad

Salat

fries

Pommes frites

fried potatoes

Bratkartoffeln

pizza

Pizza

hamburger

Hamburger

sandwich

Sandwich

escalope

Schnitzel

ham

Schinken

salami

Salami

sausage

Wurst

chicken

Huhn

roast

Braten

fish

Fisch

porridge oats

Haferflocken

muesli

Müsli

cornflakes

Cornflakes

flour

Mehl

croissant

Croissant

bread roll

Brötchen

bread

Brot

toast

Toast

cookies

Kekse

butter

Butter

curd

Quark

cake

Kuchen

egg

Ei

fried egg

Spiegelei

cheese

Käse

ice cream

Eiscreme

sugar

Zucker

honey

Honig

jelly

Marmelade

nougat cream

Nougat-Creme

curry

Curry

goat

Ziege

cow

Kuh

calf

Kalb

pig

Schwein

piglet

Ferkel

bull

Bulle

goose

Gans

duck

Ente

chick

Küken

hen

Huhn

cockerel

Hahn

rat

Ratte

cat

Katze

mouse

Maus

ox

Ochse

dog

Hund

dog house

Hundehütte

garden hose

Gartenschlauch

watering can

Gießkanne

scythe

Sense

plow

Pflug

sickle

Sichel

hoe

Hacke

pitchfork

Mistgabel

axe

Axt

pushcart

Schubkarre

trough

Trog

milk can

Milchkanne

sack

Sack

fence

Zaun

stable

Stall

greenhouse

Treibhaus

soil

Boden

seed

Saat

fertilizer

Dünger

combine harvester

Mähdrescher

harvest

ernten

harvest

Ernte

yams

Yamswurzel

wheat

Weizen

soya

Soja

potato

Kartoffel

corn

Mais

rapeseed

Raps

fruit tree

Obstbaum

manioc

Maniok

grain

Getreide

living room

Wohnzimmer

bathroom

Badezimmer

kitchen

Küche

bedroom

Schlafzimmer

kids room

Kinderzimmer

dining room

Esszimmer

floor

Boden

wall

Wand

ceiling

Decke

cellar

Keller

sauna

Sauna

balcony

Balkon

terrace

Terrasse

pool

Schwimmbad

lawn mower

Rasenmäher

sheet

Bettbezug

bedspread

Bettdecke

bed

Bett

broom

Besen

bucket

Eimer

switch

Schalter

carpet

Teppich

drape

Vorhang

table

Tisch

chair

Stuhl

rocking chair

Schaukelstuhl

armchair

Sessel

book

Buch

blanket

Decke

decoration

Dekoration

firewood

Feuerholz

film

Film

stereo system

Stereoanlage

key

Schlüssel

newspaper

Zeitung

painting

Gemälde

poster

Poster

radio

Radio

notebook

Notizblock

vacuum cleaner

Staubsauger

cactus

Kaktus

candle

Kerze

fridge
Kühlschrank

microwave oven
Mikrowelle

kitchen scales
Küchenwaage

toaster
Toaster

laundry detergent
Reinigungsmittel

stove
Backofen

freezer
Gefrierfach

dishwasher
Geschirrspüler

cooker
Herd

pot
Topf

cast-iron pot
Eisentopf

wok / kadai
Wok / Kadai

pan
Pfanne

kettle
Wasserkocher

steamer

Dampfgarer

baking tray

Backblech

crockery

Geschirr

mug

Becher

bowl

Schale

chopsticks

Essstäbchen

ladle

Suppenkelle

spatula

Pfannenwender

whisk

Schneebesen

strainer

Kochsieb

sieve

Sieb

grater

Reibe

mortar

Mörser

barbecue

Grill

fireplace

Feuerstelle

kitchen - Küche

chopping board

Schneidebrett

rolling pin

Nudelholz

corkscrew

Korkenzieher

can

Dose

can opener

Dosenöffner

oven cloth

Topflappen

sink

Waschbecken

brush

Bürste

sponge

Schwamm

blender

Mixer

deep freezer

Gefriertruhe

baby bottle

Babyflasche

tap

Wasserhahn

heating
Heizung

shower
Dusche

towel
Handtuch

shower curtain
Duschvorhang

bubble bath
Schaumbad

bathtub
Badewanne

glass
Glas

washing machine
Waschmaschine

tap
Wasserhahn

tiles
Fliesen

potty
Töpfchen

sink
Waschbecken

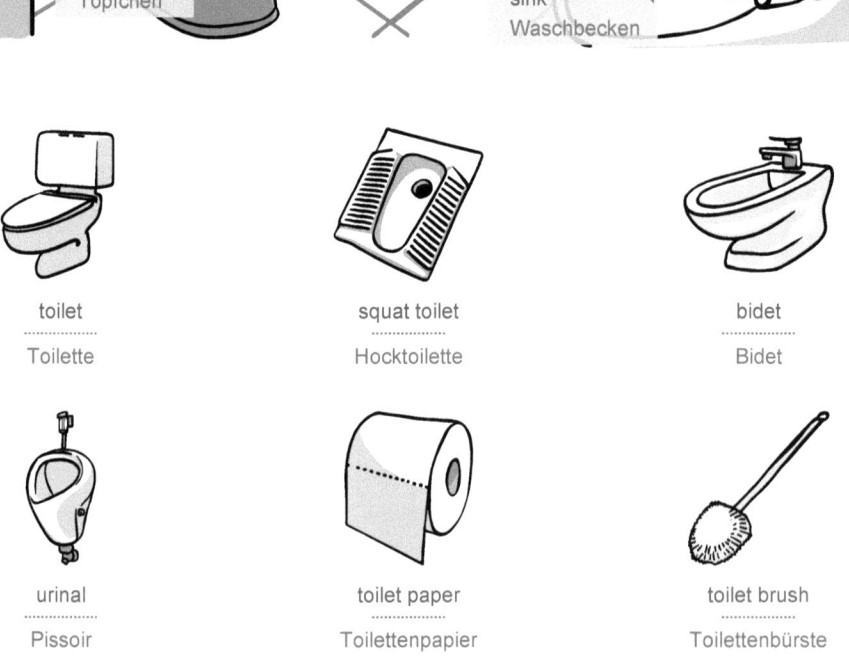

toilet	squat toilet	bidet
Toilette	Hocktoilette	Bidet
urinal	toilet paper	toilet brush
Pissoir	Toilettenpapier	Toilettenbürste

toothbrush

Zahnbürste

toothpaste

Zahnpasta

dental floss

Zahnseide

wash

waschen

hand shower

Handbrause

douche

Intimdusche

basin

Waschschüssel

back brush

Rückenbürste

soap

Seife

shower gel

Duschgel

shampoo

Shampoo

flannel

Waschlappen

drain

Abfluss

creme

Creme

deodorant

Deodorant

mirror

Spiegel

hand mirror

Kosmetikspiegel

razor

Rasierer

shaving foam

Rasierschaum

aftershave

Rasierwasser

comb

Kamm

brush

Bürste

hair-dryer

Föhn

hairspray

Haarspray

makeup

Makeup

lipstick

Lippenstift

nail varnish

Nagellack

cotton wool

Watte

nail scissors

Nagelschere

perfume

Parfum

washbag

Kulturbeutel

stool

Hocker

weighing scales

Waage

bathrobe

Bademantel

rubber gloves

Gummihandschuhe

tampon

Tampon

sanitary towel

Damenbinde

chemical toilet

Chemietoilette

alarm clock
Wecker

cuddly toy
Kuscheltier

toy car
Spielzeugauto

rattle
Rassel

doll's house
Puppenhaus

present
Geschenk

balloon

Ballon

bed

Bett

stroller

Kinderwagen

deck of cards

Kartenspiel

jigsaw

Puzzle

comic

Comic

lego bricks

Legosteine

toy blocks

Bausteine

action figure

Action Figur

romper suit

Strampelanzug

frisbee

Frisbee

mobile

Mobile

board game

Brettspiel

dice

Würfel

model train set

Modelleisenbahn

pacifier

Schnuller

party

Party

picture book

Bilderbuch

ball

Ball

doll

Puppe

play

spielen

sandpit

Sandkasten

swing

Schaukel

toys

Spielzeug

video game console

Spielkonsole

tricycle

Dreirad

teddy bear

Teddy

wardrobe

Kleiderschrank

clothing

Kleidung

socks

Socken

stockings

Strümpfe

tights

Strumpfhose

scarf
Schal

belt
Gürtel

umbrella
Regenschirm

t-shirt
T-Shirt

sneakers
Turnschuhe

boots
Stiefel

slippers
Hausschuhe

sandals

Sandalen

shoes

Schuhe

rubber boots

Gummistiefel

underwear

Unterhose

bra

Büstenhalter

undershirt

Unterhemd

body

Body

pants

Hose

jeans

Jeans

skirt

Rock

blouse

Bluse

shirt

Hemd

pullover

Pullover

sweater

Kapuzenpullover

blazer

Blazer

jacket

Jacke

coat

Mantel

raincoat

Regenmantel

costume

Kostüm

dress

Kleid

wedding dress

Hochzeitskleid

suit

Anzug

nightgown

Nachthemd

pajamas

Schlafanzug

sari

Sari

headscarf

Kopftuch

turban

Turban

burka

Burka

kaftan

Kaftan

abaya

Abaya

swimsuit

Badeanzug

trunks

Badehose

shorts

Kurze Hose

tracksuit

Trainingsanzug

apron

Schürze

gloves

Handschuhe

clothing - Kleidung

button

Knopf

glasses

Brille

bracelet

Armband

necklace

Halskette

ring

Ring

earring

Ohrring

cap

Mütze

coat hanger

Kleiderbügel

hat

Hut

tie

Krawatte

zip

Reißverschluss

helmet

Helm

braces

Hosenträger

school uniform

Schuluniform

uniform

Uniform

bib

Lätzchen

pacifier

Schnuller

diaper

Windel

server
Server

filing cabinet
Aktenschrank

printer
Drucker

monitor
Monitor

paper
Papier

mouse
Maus

desk
Schreibtisch

folder
Ordner

keyboard
Tastatur

waste-paper basket
Papierkorb

chair
Stuhl

computer
Computer

coffee mug

Kaffeebecher

calculator

Taschenrechner

internet

Internet

laptop

Laptop

letter

Brief

message

Nachricht

cell phone

Handy

network

Netzwerk

photocopier

Kopierer

software

Software

telephone

Telefon

plug socket

Steckdose

fax machine

Fax

form

Formular

document

Dokument

buy
kaufen

pay
bezahlen

trade
handeln

money
Geld

USD

dollar
Dollar

EUR

euro
Euro

JPY

yen
Yen

RUB

rouble
Rubel

CHF

Swiss franc
Franken

CNY

renminbi yuan
Renminbi Yuan

INR

rupee
Rupie

cash point
Geldautomat

currency exchange office

Wechselstube

gold

Gold

silver

Silber

oil

Öl

energy

Energie

price

Preis

contract

Vertrag

tax

Steuer

stock

Aktie

work

arbeiten

employee

Angestellter

employer

Arbeitgeber

factory

Fabrik

shop

Geschäft

economy - Wirtschaft

police officer
Polizist

fireman
Feuerwehrmann

cook
Koch

doctor
Arzt

pilot
Pilot

gardener
Gärtner

carpenter
Tischler

seamstress
Näherin

judge
Richter

chemist
Chemiker

actor
Schauspieler

bus driver

Busfahrer

taxi driver

Taxifahrer

fisherman

Fischer

cleaning lady

Putzfrau

roofer

Dachdecker

waiter

Kellner

hunter

Jäger

painter

Maler

baker

Bäcker

electrician

Elektriker

builder

Bauarbeiter

engineer

Ingenieur

butcher

Schlachter

plumber

Klempner

postman

Postbote

soldier

Soldat

architect

Architekt

cashier

Kassierer

florist

Florist

hairdresser

Friseur

conductor

Schaffner

mechanic

Mechaniker

captain

Kapitän

dentist

Zahnarzt

scientist

Wissenschaftler

rabbi

Rabbi

imam

Imam

monk

Mönch

pastor

Geistlicher

occupations - Berufe

hammer
Hammer

pliers
Zange

screwdriver
Schraubendreher

wrench
Schraubenschlüssel

torch
Taschenlampe

excavator

Bagger

toolbox

Werkzeugkasten

ladder

Leiter

saw

Säge

nails

Nägel

drill

Bohrer

repair
reparieren

shovel
Schaufel

Damn!
Mist!

dustpan
Kehrblech

paint can
Farbtopf

screws
Schrauben

musical instruments
Musikinstrumente

loud speaker
Lautsprecher

drum set
Schlagzeug

guitar
Gitarre

double bass
Kontrabass

trumpet
Trompete

piano

Klavier

violin

Violine

bass

Bass

timpani

Pauke

drums

Trommeln

keyboard

Keyboard

saxophone

Saxophon

flute

Flöte

microphone

Mikrofon

entrance
Eingang

tiger
Tiger

cage
Käfig

zebra
Zebra

animal feed
Tierfutter

panda
Panda

animals

Tiere

elephant

Elefant

kangaroo

Känguru

rhino

Nashorn

gorilla

Gorilla

bear

Bär

camel

Kamel

ostrich

Strauß

lion

Löwe

monkey

Affe

flamingo

Flamingo

parrot

Papagei

polar bear

Eisbär

penguin

Pinguin

shark

Hai

peacock

Pfau

snake

Schlange

crocodile

Krokodil

zookeeper

Zoowärter

seal

Robbe

jaguar

Jaguar

pony

Pony

leopard

Leopard

hippo

Nilpferd

giraffe

Giraffe

eagle

Adler

boar

Wildschwein

fish

Fisch

turtle

Schildkröte

walrus

Walross

fox

Fuchs

gazelle

Gazelle

American football
American Football

cycling
Radfahren

tennis
Tennis

basketball
Basketball

swimming
Schwimmen

boxing
Boxen

ice hockey
Eishockey

soccer
Fußball

badminton
Badminton

athletics
Leichtathletik

handball
Handball

skiing
Skilaufen

polo
Polo

jump
springen

hug
umarmen

laugh
lachen

walk
gehen

sing
singen

pray
beten

kiss
küssen

dream
träumen

write

schreiben

draw

zeichnen

show

zeigen

push

drücken

give

geben

take

nehmen

have
haben

do
tun

be
sein

stand
stehen

run
laufen

pull
ziehen

throw
werfen

fall
fallen

lie
liegen

wait
warten

carry
tragen

sit
sitzen

get dressed
anziehen

sleep
schlafen

wake up
aufwachen

look at

ansehen

cry

weinen

stroke

streicheln

comb

kämmen

talk

reden

understand

verstehen

ask

fragen

listen

hören

drink

trinken

eat

essen

tidy up

aufräumen

love

lieben

cook

kochen

drive

fahren

fly

fliegen

sail

segeln

calculate

rechnen

read

lesen

learn

lernen

work

arbeiten

marry

heiraten

sew

nähen

brush teeth

Zähne putzen

kill

töten

smoke

rauchen

send

senden

grandmother
Großmutter

grandfather
Großvater

father
Vater

mother
Mutter

baby
Baby

daughter
Tochter

son
Sohn

guest

Gast

aunt

Tante

uncle

Onkel

brother

Bruder

sister

Schwester

forehead
Stirn

eye
Auge

shoulder
Schulter

finger
Finger

face
Gesicht

chin
Kinn

hand
Hand

breast
Brust

leg
Bein

arm
Arm

baby

Baby

man

Mann

woman

Frau

girl

Mädchen

boy

Junge

head

Kopf

back

Rücken

belly

Bauch

navel

Nabel

toe

Zeh

heel

Ferse

bone

Knochen

hip

Hüfte

knee

Knie

elbow

Ellenbogen

nose

Nase

buttocks

Gesäß

skin

Haut

cheek

Wange

ear

Ohr

lip

Lippe

body - Körper

mouth

Mund

tooth

Zahn

tongue

Zunge

brain

Gehirn

heart

Herz

muscle

Muskel

lung

Lunge

liver

Leber

stomach

Magen

kidneys

Nieren

sex

Geschlechtsverkehr

condom

Kondom

ovum

Eizelle

semen

Sperma

pregnancy

Schwangerschaft

menstruation

Menstruation

vagina

Vagina

penis

Penis

eyebrow

Augenbraue

hair

Haar

neck

Hals

hospital
Krankenhaus

ambulance
Krankenwagen

wheelchair
Rollstuhl

fracture
Bruch

doctor

Arzt

emergency room

Notaufnahme

nurse

Krankenschwester

emergency

Notfall

unconscious

ohnmächtig

pain

Schmerz

injury

Verletzung

bleeding

Blutung

heart attack

Herzinfarkt

stroke

Schlaganfall

allergy

Allergie

cough

Husten

fever

Fieber

flu

Grippe

diarrhea

Durchfall

headache

Kopfschmerzen

cancer

Krebs

diabetes

Diabetis

surgeon

Chirurg

scalpel

Skalpell

operation

Operation

CT
CT

x-ray
Röntgen

ultrasound
Ultraschall

face mask
Maske

disease
Krankheit

waiting room
Wartezimmer

crutch
Krücke

plaster
Pflaster

bandage
Verband

injection
Injektion

stethoscope
Stethoskop

stretcher
Trage

clinical thermometer
Thermometer

birth
Geburt

overweight
Übergewicht

hearing aid

Hörgerät

disinfectant

Desinfektionsmittel

infection

Infektion

virus

Virus

HIV / AIDS

HIV / AIDS

medicine

Medizin

vaccination

Impfung

tablets

Tabletten

pill

Pille

emergency call

Notruf

blood pressure monitor

Blutdruck-Messgerät

ill / healthy

krank / gesund

Help!

Hilfe!

alarm

Alarm

assault

Überfall

attack

Angriff

danger

Gefahr

emergency exit

Notausgang

Fire!

Feuer!

fire extinguisher

Feuerlöscher

accident

Unfall

first-aid kit

Erste-Hilfe-Koffer

SOS

SOS

police

Polizei

Europe

Europa

North America

Nordamerika

South America

Südamerika

Africa

Afrika

Asia

Asien

Australia

Australien

Atlantic

Atlantik

Pacific

Pazifik

Indian Ocean

Indischer Ozean

Antarctic Ocean

Antarktischer Ozean

Arctic Ocean

Arktischer Ozean

North pole

Nordpol

South pole

Südpol

Antarctica

Antarktis

earth

Erde

land

Land

sea

Meer

island

Insel

nation

Nation

state

Staat

clock face
Zifferblatt

hour hand
Stundenzeiger

minute hand
Minutenzeiger

second hand
Sekundenzeiger

What time is it?
Wie spät ist es?

day
Tag

time
Zeit

now
jetzt

digital watch
Digitaluhr

minute
Minute

hour
Stunde

week

Woche

yesterday

gestern

today

heute

tomorrow

morgen

morning

Morgen

noon

Mittag

evening

Abend

MO	TU	WE	TH	FR	SA	SU
1	2	3	4	5	6	7
8	9	10	11	12	13	14
15	16	17	18	19	20	21
22	23	24	25	26	27	28
29	30	31	1	2	3	4

workdays

Arbeitstage

MO	TU	WE	TH	FR	SA	SU
1	2	3	4	5	6	7
8	9	10	11	12	13	14
15	16	17	18	19	20	21
22	23	24	25	26	27	28
29	30	31	1	2	3	4

weekend

Wochenende

rain
Regen

snow
Schnee

wind
Wind

spring
Frühling

fall
Herbst

summer
Sommer

winter
Winter

weather forecast

Wettervorhersage

thermometer

Thermometer

sunshine

Sonnenschein

cloud

Wolke

fog

Nebel

humidity

Luftfeuchtigkeit

lightning

Blitz

thunder

Donner

storm

Sturm

hail

Hagel

monsoon

Monsun

flood

Flut

ice

Eis

January

Januar

February

Februar

March

März

April

April

May

Mai

June

Juni

July

Juli

August

August

year - Jahr

September

September

October

Oktober

November

November

December

Dezember

shapes

Formen

circle

Kreis

square

Quadrat

rectangle

Rechteck

triangle

Dreieck

sphere

Kugel

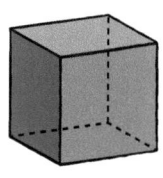

cube

Würfel

colors

Farben

white

weiß

yellow

gelb

orange

orange

pink

pink

red

rot

purple

lila

blue

blau

green

grün

brown

braun

gray

grau

black

schwarz

a lot / a little

viel / wenig

angry / calm

wütend / friedlich

beautiful / ugly

hübsch / hässlich

beginning / end

Anfang / Ende

big / small

groß / klein

bright / dark

hell / dunkel

brother / sister

Bruder / Schwester

clean / dirty

sauber / schmutzig

complete / incomplete

vollständig / unvollständig

day / night

Tag / Nacht

dead / alive

tot / lebendig

wide / narrow

breit / schmal

edible / inedible

genießbar / ungenießbar

evil / kind

böse / freundlich

excited / bored

aufgeregt / gelangweilt

fat / thin

dick / dünn

first / last

zuerst / zuletzt

friend / enemy

Freund / Feind

full / empty

voll / leer

hard / soft

hart / weich

heavy / light

schwer / leicht

hunger / thirst

Hunger / Durst

ill / healthy

krank / gesund

illegal / legal

illegal / legal

intelligent / stupid

intelligent / dumm

left / right

links / rechts

near / far

nah / fern

new / used
neu / gebraucht

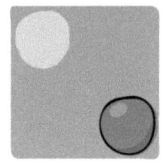

nothing / something
nichts / etwas

old / young
alt / jung

on / off
an / aus

open / closed
offen / geschlossen

quiet / loud
leise / laut

rich / poor
reich / arm

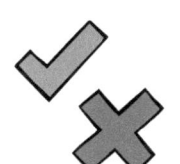

right / wrong
richtig / falsch

rough / smooth
rau / glatt

sad / happy
traurig / glücklich

short / long
kurz / lang

slow / fast
langsam / schnell

wet / dry
nass / trocken

warm / cool
warm / kühl

war / peace
Krieg / Frieden

Zahlen

0

zero

null

1

one

eins

2

two

zwei

3

three

drei

4

four

vier

5

five

fünf

6

six

sechs

7

seven

sieben

8

eight

acht

9

nine

neun

10

ten

zehn

11

eleven

elf

12

twelve

zwölf

13

thirteen

dreizehn

14

fourteen

vierzehn

15

fifteen

fünfzehn

16

sixteen

sechzehn

17

seventeen

siebzehn

18

eighteen

achtzehn

19

nineteen

neunzehn

20

twenty

zwanzig

100

hundred

hundert

1.000

thousand

tausend

1.000.000

million

million

English
Englisch

American English
Amerikanisches Englisch

Chinese Mandarin
Chinesisch Mandarin

Hindi
Hindi

Spanish
Spanisch

French
Französisch

Arabic
Arabisch

Russian
Russisch

Portuguese
Portugiesisch

Bengali
Bengalisch

German
Deutsch

Japanese
Japanisch

I
ich

you
du

he / she / it
er / sie / es

we
wir

you
ihr

they
sie

who?
wer?

what?
was?

how?
wie?

where?
wo?

when?
wann?

HELLO, I AM

name
Name

behind

hinter

in

in

in front of

vor

over

über

on

auf

under

unter

beside

neben

between

zwischen

place

Ort